# AGE WORDS:
## A GLOSSARY
## ON HEALTH AND AGING

D0925368

# Table of Contents

# Introduction

A ging and the problems of older people have gained wide recognition only within the past 20 years. In this time, the relatively new field of gerontology has developed rapidly and evolved a special vocabulary of its own. The terms used to describe the aging process reflect many disciplines, ranging from medicine and social services to housing and law.

*Age Words* is a collection of common terms used by gerontologists, but with an emphasis on health and research. An effort was made to define the terms in a form consistent with common usage. Yet in a field still changing rapidly, professionals who study the various areas of aging occasionally give the same word a slightly different meaning. For example, city and government planners may define "aged" according to chronological years (age 60 or 65) while biomedical scientists may base the definition on physiological processes.

The glossary is intended for a broad audience—for older persons and their families, students of aging, librarians, medical writers, allied health professionals, and others with a special interest in the field.

How do you look up a word? Related terms are grouped under subject categories: aging, research on aging, the body, medicines and drugs, medical problems, women, mental health, social problems and services, and medical specialties. These are listed in the table of contents. You can also look up words by referring to the index at the back of the glossary.

Word pronunciations accompany many of the terms. They are divided into syllables, and the syllables are marked with an accent (´) to indicate the primary or greater stress and a line over the vowel (ā) to indicate a long vowel sound.

**age segregation**

The separation of people based on age—as in retirement communities or senior citizens' centers.

**aged**
*(ā' jid)*

The state of being old. A person may be defined as aged on the basis of having reached a specific age—for example, 65 is often used for social or legislative policies while 75 is used for physiological evaluations.

**ageism**
*(āj' izm)*

Prejudice against people because they are old. Ageism implies a broader meaning than gerontophobia, the unreasonable fear and hatred of older persons. The term was coined by Robert N. Butler, M.D., first Director of the National Institute on Aging.

**aging**
*(ā' jing)*

The changes that occur normally in plants and animals as they grow older. Some age changes begin at birth and continue until death; other changes begin at maturity and end at death. Also see aging research (page 11).

**centenarian**
*(sen-tnar' ē-un)*

A person who is 100 years or older. There were 2,300 centenarians identified in the 1980 U.S. census.

**chronological age**
*(kron-o-loj' i-kal)*

An individual's numerical age dating from the time of his or her birth. Compare functional age (page 8).

**elderly or elder**

Generally referring to individuals over age

60. Other terms used to describe certain groups of older people are

*frail elderly.* Elderly persons whose physical and emotional abilities or social support system is so reduced that maintaining a household or social contacts is difficult and sometimes impossible, without regular assistance from others. Healthy persons are usually not in this group until after age 75; and even then many are not frail until they reach very late years, such as beyond age 90.

*functionally dependent elderly.* Individuals whose illnesses, disabilities, or social problems have reduced their ability to perform self-care and household tasks in an independent manner.

**functional age**

An assessment of age based on physical or mental performance rather than on the number of years since birth. Compare chronological age (page 7).

**geriatric medicine**

Also called geriatrics. The medical knowledge of physical disability in older persons—including the diagnosis, treatment, and prevention of disorders. Geriatric medicine recognizes aging as a normal process, not a disease state.

**geriatric psychiatry**

See psychiatry (page 48).

**geriatrician**
*(jer-ē-a-tri' shun)*

Physicians with special training in geriatric medicine. In earlier years this training was self-taught through the special attention physicians gave their older patients. Now, 1- to 3-year training programs, which follow the regular medical curriculum, are established in a number of teaching medical centers.

**geriatrics**
*(jer-ē-a' triks)*

Refers to geriatric medicine. The term was originally coined in 1909 by the American physician Ingnaz L. Nascher when he recognized a similarity between the fields of aging and pediatrics. Nascher is the founder of modern geriatrics in the U.S.

**gerontology**
*(jer-un-tol' o-jē)*

The study of aging from the broadest perspective. Gerontologists examine not only the clinical and biological aspects of aging but also psychosocial, economic, and historical conditions. Elie Metchnikoff, of the Pasteur Institute in Paris, first used the term in 1903 to describe the biological study of senescence.

**senescence**
*(se-nes' sens)*

Aging. The normal process of growing old, a process that occurs continuously at every biological level (chemical, cellular, tissue, organ systems, and organism).

# Research on Aging

| | |
|---|---|
| **aging research** | The study of the interrelating factors that affect aging—clinical medicine, social and psychological relations, and environmental conditions. Aging research attempts to distinguish the changes occurring normally during aging from changes caused by illness, heredity, or the environment. |
| **behavioral sciences** | The study of human development, values, and interpersonal relations. The behavioral sciences encompass such fields as psychiatry, psychology, cultural anthropology, sociology, and political science. |
| **biometry** *(bī-om' i-trē)* | The mathematical study of biological facts about a subject. A statistical examination of biological data—for example, the calculation of life expectancy. |
| **cohort** *(kō' hort)* | A group of people who are born at the same period of time or who enter a system, such as a nursing home, at the same time. One type of research design compares cohorts to see if there are differences in the way they grow older. |
| **demography** *(di-mog' re-fē)* | The study of a population and those variables bringing about change in that population. Variables studied by demographers are age, sex, race, education, income, geographic trends, birth, and death. See epidemiology (page 12), biometry (above). |

**dependency ratio**    A comparison between those individuals whom society considers economically productive and those it considers economically unproductive. Since many people over 65 are retired from the work force, this group is usually classified as economically unproductive (others in this category are children and nonworking individuals between ages 18 and 64).

**epidemiology**    The study of the frequency and
*(ep-a-dē-mē-ol'o-jē)*    distribution of illness in a population. Terms used by epidemiologists include

*endemic (en-dem'ik)*. Found in a particular geographic area or among a particular group of people.

*epidemic (ep-a-dem'ik)*. Spreading rapidly among many individuals in an area, especially a contagious disease.

*pandemic (pan-dem'ik)*. Occurring over a large geographic area—universal or worldwide.

**incidence**    How frequently a disease occurs. The rate of new cases occurring in a population during a given period of time. Compare prevalence (page 14).

**life cycle**    The entire course of a person's life—from infancy to old age. Health, social roles and expectations, and socioeconomic status tend to change as an individual moves from one phase of life to the next.

| | |
|---|---|
| **life expectancy** | A statistical projection of the number of years an individual is expected to live. Life expectancy can be calculated from birth (for example, a person born in 1984 could be expected to live to age 74), or it can be calculated from some other point (such as the number of years a person could expect to live after reaching a given age). Persons of the same age can have different life expectancies depending on their race, sex, or socioeconomic circumstances. |
| **life span** | The years a human being could live if negative variables, such as disease or accidents, did not shorten the number. An ideal number, probably approaching 110 years. |
| **longevity**<br>*(lon-jev' i-tē)* | The condition or quality of being long-lived. |
| **longitudinal research** | Studies that examine one group of individuals over a long period of time—as they grow, develop, and age. This is in contrast to cross-sectional research in which individuals of different ages are compared with one another at one point in time. |
| **minority group** | A small number of people within a society. Members of racial minority groups who are elderly bear a double burden of discrimination based on both race and age. |

**morbidity rate**
*(mor-bid´ i-tē)*

The ratio of individuals who are ill or disabled to the total number within a population.

**mortality rate**
*(mor-tal´ i-tē)*

Death rate. The ratio of individuals who have died to the total number of individuals in the population during a given period of time. The deaths of 100 individuals in a population of 1,000 would result in a mortality rate of 100.

**National Institute on Aging (NIA)**

One of the National Institutes of Health, the NIA was established by Congress on May 31, 1974 (Public Law 93-296). As a Federal agency, the NIA supports research on conditions that affect the aging process. Institute activities range from investigations on biological, social, and psychological issues to training personnel for related research.

**prevalence**
*(prev´ a-lenz)*

The total number of individuals in a given population who have a specific disorder at one period in time. Compare incidence (page 12).

**psychosocial research on aging**

The scientific investigation of individual characteristics (intellectual ability, personality, attitudes, and behaviors) and social environments (family relationships and work situations) as they influence the way people age.

**teaching nursing home**

A nursing home affiliated with a university medical school or medical center. In addition to the "teaching" function of the teaching nursing home, another of its purposes is to conduct research on the chronic health problems that often lead older persons to be institutionalized (problems such as dementia, incontinence, loss of mobility, depression, and sleep disorders).

# The Body

## Bones:

**contracture**
*(kon' trak-tur)*

Progressive stiffening in the muscles, tendons, and ligaments that surround the joints. Contractures tend to develop after a stroke or an injury when prolonged immobility has limited the movement of joints.

**orthopedics**
*(or-tho-pē' diks)*

The medical knowledge, diagnosis, and treatment of the skeletal system (the bones, joints, muscles, ligaments, and tendons).

**osteoporosis**
*(os' tē-ō-po-rō' sis)*

A decrease in density of the bones causing structural weakness throughout the skeleton. Fractures can result from even a minor injury or fall. Some bone loss occurs normally in older adults, but osteoporosis develops most often in white women after menopause. See menopause (page 46).

**rheumatology**
*(ru-ma-tol' o-jē)*

The medical study of rheumatic diseases; the diagnosis and treatment of inflammatory diseases (rheumatoid arthritis, for example) and disease in the musculoskeletal system (bones, joints, and muscles). See arthritis (page 35).

## Brain:

**Alzheimer disease**
*(altz' hī-mer)*

A form of dementia first described in 1906 by German neurologist Alois Alzheimer.

Alzheimer disease produces severe intellectual deterioration in older persons and is currently considered an irreversible disease. See dementia (below).

**aphasia**
*(a-fā' zha)*

Loss of the ability to use or understand language.

**central nervous system**

The brain and spinal cord.

**cognitive**
*(kog' ni-tiv)*

Refers to the mental processes of comprehension, memory, judgment, and reasoning—as opposed to emotional processes.

**computerized axial tomogram (CT or CAT scan)**
*(kom-pu' te-rīzd ak' sē-al tō' mo-gram)*

A medical test producing colored images or a "map" of the structure of the body being investigated. A painless procedure, CT scans are used in evaluating patients for tumors, a loss in brain tissue (stroke), or brain disease (Alzheimer disease).

**delirium**
*(di-lēr' ē-um)*

A mental state in which one experiences confusion and decreased awareness of surroundings. A delirium may be caused by fever, alcohol or drug intoxication, head injury, or some other medical disorder. It develops rapidly (onset is acute) but can usually be treated successfully.

**dementia**
*(di-men' sha)*

The severe impairment of cognitive functions (thinking, memory, and personality). Of our elderly population, 5 to 6 percent have dementia. Alzheimer disease causes approximately one-half of these cases, vascular disorders (multiple strokes) cause one-fourth, and the other dementias are caused by alcoholism, heart disease, infections, endocrine disorders, toxic reactions to medicines, and other rarer conditions. While impairment from Alzheimer disease and vascular disorders is permanent, dementia caused by other conditions can usually be corrected.

**electroencephalo-graph (EEG)**
*(i-lek-trō-en-sef'*
*a-le-graf)*

An instrument used to record electrical impulses in the brain. Electrodes are attached (painlessly) to the scalp to record impulses, and these impulses are registered on graph paper as a brain wave pattern. An EEG is used to identify brain damage, tumors, or neurological disorders such as epilepsy.

**plaques**
*(plaks)*

Certain areas of the brain that have undergone a specific form of degeneration. Plaques are usually found in patients with Alzheimer disease, although they are also found to a lesser extent in older persons who are normal.

**senile dementia**
*(sē' nīl*
*di-men' sha)*

An outdated term for dementia. Years ago dementia was thought to be part of normal aging, but now we know that most people do not become demented as they grow older and that dementia, when it occurs, is due to some specific disease process. See dementia (page 18).

19

**senility**
*(si-nil´i-tē)*

An outdated term referring to abnormal deterioration in the mental functions of old people. See dementia (page 18).

**stroke**
*(strōk´)*

Also called cerebrovascular accident. Disruption in the supply of blood to some part of the brain causing sudden damage to the brain. The outcome of a stroke can vary depending on the cause. Possible outcomes are paralysis, loss of sensation, incontinence, impaired speech and thinking, and sometimes death. Rehabilitation therapy can help stroke patients regain their ability to move and function. See rehabilitation therapy (page 53).

# Ears, Nose, and Throat:

**otorhinolaryn-gology**
*(o-tō-rī-nō-lar-ing-gol´o-jē)*

The medical study of the ears, nose, and throat—abbreviated ENT.

**otosclerosis**
*(o-tō-skle-rō´sis)*

A pathologic change that occurs in the middle and inner ear, causing progressive impairment in hearing.

**presbycusis**
*(prez-bē-ku´sis)*

The most common type of hearing loss in people over 65. Presbycusis results in a gradual decline in the ability to hear high-pitched sounds or to distinguish consonants in speech, which sometimes causes an older person to misinterpret what is being said.

# Eyes:

**bifocals**

Eyeglass lenses that correct both short-and long-range vision.

**cataract**
*(kat' a-rakt)*

A cloudiness or opacity ·that develops in the lens of the eye and results in poorer vision. Previously one of the leading causes of blindness in persons over 60, cataracts can now be surgically removed.

**diabetic retinopathy**
*(dī-ah-be' tik ret-i-nop' ah-thē)*

A disorder of the blood vessels in the retina (tissue that transmits visual impulses to the brain). The condition develops most often in older diabetics who have had the condition for many years. Diabetic retinopathy causes blurred vision or it can block vision (from broken blood vessels leaking into the retina) or it can lead to blindness—though blindness can sometimes be averted through early detection. See diabetes (page 37).

**glaucoma**
*(glaw-kō' ma)*

A disease in which pressure builds up within the eye and causes internal damage, gradually destroying vision. Often hereditary, glaucoma usually affects persons after age 40. Symptoms may be blurred vision, difficulty in focusing, loss of peripheral vision, or slow adaptation to dark. Often there are no symptoms until severe and irreversible loss of vision has occurred. While no method exists for preventing glaucoma, diagnosing the disease in its earliest stages can prevent further damage.

**macular degeneration**
*(mak' u-lar di-jen-er-ā' shun)*

Progressive, irreversible damage to the macula (part of the retina) which results in a gradual loss of fine, reading vision and eventually blindness. The use of lasers, a new form of therapy, can in some instances halt the degeneration.

**myopia**
*(mi-ō' pē-a)*

Nearsightedness.

**ophthalmology**
*(of-thal-mol' o-jē)*

The medical study of the structure, function, and diseases of the eye. Ophthalmologists are doctors of medicine (M.D.) or doctors of osteopathy (D.O.) who perform all types of eye surgery as well as prescribe corrective lenses and medicines for the eye.

**optician**
*(op-tish' an)*

A person who makes corrective lenses according to the prescription of an ophthalmologist or optometrist, but who does not examine eyes.

**optometry**
*(op-tom' i-trē)*

Profession of testing the eyes for defects in vision for the purpose of prescribing corrective glasses. An optometrist is a doctor of optometry (O.D.), not an M.D. or a D.O. Compare ophthalmology (above).

**presbyopia**
*(prez-bē-ō′ pē-a)*

Reduction in the ability to see at close range. This is due to the gradual loss of elasticity in the lens of the eye which occurs throughout life, but does not become apparent until the mid-forties.

## *Heart and Circulation:*

**angina pectoris**
*(an-ji′nah or*
*an′ ji-nah*
*pek′ tōr-is)*

Chest pain—often a symptom of impending heart attack. Angina attacks usually occur after some physical or emotional exertion. The coronary arteries (those arteries supplying the heart muscle with oxygen and nutrients) are narrowed by atherosclerosis which prevents the heart from receiving a sufficient supply of blood.

**arteriosclerosis**
*(ar-ter-ē-ō-skle-*
*rō′ sis)*

Hardening of the arteries. It can be caused by a number of diseases in which the inner walls of the arteries thicken and lose elasticity, reducing the flow of blood through the vessels. Arteriosclerosis is the major cause of cardiovascular disease.

**atherosclerosis**
*(ath-er-ō-skle-*
*rō′ sis)*

One type of arteriosclerosis. Atherosclerosis causes atheroma (deposits of fat or plaque) to form on the inner walls of the arteries, decreasing the width of the blood vessel. The danger of atherosclerosis is that the accumulated atheroma can eventually block the flow of blood, triggering a heart attack or stroke. See arteriosclerosis (above), plaque (page 26).

**blood pressure**

The pressure of the blood against the walls of the arteries. Blood pressure is generally expressed by two numbers such as 120/80. The higher number is the systolic pressure (the contraction of the heart which puts the greatest pressure on the vessel) and the lower number is the diastolic pressure (the period of relaxation). The normal blood pressure of a healthy older person is often higher than the pressure of a younger person.

**blood vessels**

The vascular system (arteries, capillaries, and veins). The vessels through which blood circulates in the body.

*artery (ar' ter-ē)*. The arteries carry blood away from the heart to the various organs in order to deliver fresh oxygen and nutrients.

*capillary (kap' i-lar-ē)*. The smallest blood vessels. Capillaries are fragile, thin-walled vessels that form a bridge linking arteries with veins. They receive oxygen and glucose-rich blood from the arteries, transport this blood to body cells, and receive back waste products (such as carbon dioxide)—finally carrying the blood to the veins.

*vein (vān)*. The veins return the blood from various parts of the body to the heart.

**cardiology**
*(kar-dē-ol' o-jē)*

The medical study of the structure, function, and diseases of the heart and blood vessels.

**cardiopulmonary resuscitation (CPR)**
*(kar-dē-ō-pul' mo-ner-ē rē-sus-i-tā' shun)*

An emergency procedure used when a heart attack is occurring and blood circulation or breathing has stopped (a cardiopulmonary arrest).

**circulatory system**
*(sur' kū-la-tor-ē)*

The heart, blood vessels, and circulation of the blood throughout the body.

**electrocardiograph (ECG or EKG)**
*(i-lek-trō-kar' dē-a-graf)*

An instrument that measures electrical impulses generated by the heart. Wires are placed on the outside of the chest near the heart to record impulses which are in turn transformed to paper as wave patterns, called an electrocardiogram.

**heart attack**

Damage to an area of the heart muscle (myocardium) due to an insufficient supply of blood. Various symptoms can indicate a heart attack is about to occur—for example, chest pain (angina pectoris), sweating, nausea, shortness of breath, and weakness; moreover, in older people there are sometimes no symptoms. Other terms that refer to a heart attack are myocardial infarction, infarction, coronary occlusion, coronary thrombosis, or coronary.

**hematology**
*(hē-ma-tol' o-jē)*

The study of the function and diseases of the blood.

**hypertension**
*(hi-pur-ten' shun)*

High blood pressure. Blood pressure that is repeatedly elevated above a normal

25

range. Left untreated, hypertension can increase the risk of heart attack, stroke, or kidney damage.

**infarct**
*(in ' farkt)*

The area of tissue that is damaged (or dies) from receiving too little blood.

**myocardial infarction**
*(mī-ō-kar' dē-al in-fark' shun)*

Heart attack.

**pacemaker**

A small group of specialized cells in the heart that produce electrical impulses to start heart contractions. An "artificial pacemaker" is an electrical device used as a substitute for the heart's natural pacemaker and controls heartbeats through a series of electrical discharges. An artificial pacemaker may be placed on the outside of the chest or implanted within the chest wall.

**plaque**
*(plak)*

Also called atheroma. Plaque is a fatty substance that builds up inside artery walls and causes blood vessels to narrow. It develops as part of atherosclerosis. See atherosclerosis (page 23).

**sphygmomanometer**
*(sfig-mō-ma-nom' e-ter)*

A device used for measuring blood pressure.

**varicose veins**
*(var' i-kōs)*

Varicose veins develop from the heavy pressure of blood against walls of the veins, usually after many years. While there are several types of varicose veins, the most common develop on the calves just under the skin surface. These veins sometimes look prominent but only rarely cause a problem.

# Kidneys and Urinary System:

**benign prostatic hypertrophy (BPH)**
(bi-nīn' pros-ta' tik hī-per' tro-fē)

An enlargement of the prostate. BPH is caused by the general enlargement of the prostate or by small, noncancerous tumors that grow inside. An enlarged prostate sometimes obstructs the urinary flow, which prostatectomy can relieve. See prostate (below), prostatectomy (page 28).

**incontinence**
(in-kon' ti-nens)

Lacking voluntary control over the bladder or bowel. In most people incontinence can be treated and controlled, if not cured. Specific changes in body function, often resulting from disease or the use of medications, are the cause of incontinence.

**nephrology**
(nef-rol' o-jē)

The medical study of the structure, function, and diseases of the kidneys.

**prostate**
(pros' tāt)

In men, a gland surrounding the base of the urethra. Its purpose is not fully understood but appears related to sexual function. Cancer of the prostate becomes more likely with advancing age; at the same time it is one of the easier types of cancer to treat.

**prostatectomy**
*(pros-ta-tek'*
*to-mē)*

The surgical removal of the prostate gland. The operation is common in older men since the prostate gland normally enlarges somewhat and may eventually interfere with urination. Men usually can resume normal sexual activity soon after the operation.

**renal**
*(rēn' l)*

Having to do with the kidneys.

**urology**
*(ū-rol' o-jē)*

The medical study of the structure, function, and diseases of the urinary system (bladder and kidneys) in both men and women, and of the male reproductive system.

## Skin:

**age spots**

Also called liver spots or senile lentigines. Age spots are dark brown and resemble large freckles. Although these spots appear in older people, aging is not their primary cause; instead, age spots develop from exposure over many years to the sun's ultraviolet radiation.

**decubitus ulcer**
*(de-kū' bi-tus*
*ul' ser)*

Also called bed sores or pressure sores. Decubitus ulcers develop when the skin overlying a bony prominence of the body is subjected to prolonged, unrelieved pressure. The most common cause of these ulcers is a long stay in bed without changing the position of the body.

| **dermatology** (dur-ma-tol' a-jē) | The medical study of the structure, function, and diseases of the skin. |
| --- | --- |
| **ulcer** (ul' ser) | A break or sore on the skin surface or on internal tissues that line the body (such as the digestive tract). |
| **wrinkles** | A condition caused by atrophy and elastic-tissue changes in the skin. Some wrinkles develop in the normal course of aging, but severe wrinkling comes from repeated exposure to the sun. No cream, oil, or facial exercise can permanently smooth or remove them; only cosmetic surgery can produce a long-lasting effect on the appearance of wrinkles. |

## Stomach (Digestion):

| **constipation** (kon-sti-pā' shun) | A decrease in the frequency of bowel movements, usually accompanied by the prolonged or difficult passage of stools. Causes might be poor diet, decreased fluid intake, or incorrect use of laxatives. Normal bowel movements range from two a day to one every 3 days. |
| --- | --- |
| **dehydration** (de-hi-dra' shun) | A loss of the body's normal water content which can affect both physical and mental functions. Individuals with brain, kidney, or gastrointestinal disease may find it |

difficult to maintain a normal amount of water in the body without the aid of medications.

**diarrhea**
*(dī-a-rē′ a)*

Loose or watery stools and an increase in bowel movements, usually more than two a day. Diarrhea is a common symptom of gastrointestinal disease (a disorder of the stomach and intestines).

**gastroenterology**
*(gas-trō-en-te-rol′ o-jē)*

The medical study of the structure, function, and diseases of the digestive tract, the stomach, and the intestines.

**nutrition**
*(nu-tri′ shun)*

Pertaining to the body's need for food (protein, fat, carbohydrate, vitamins, and minerals). The nutritional needs of older people may be somewhat different from those of younger people.

**proctology**
*(prok-tol′ o-jē)*

The medical study of the rectum and anus.

# Medicines and Drugs

**analgesic**
(n-al-jē' zik)

A drug, such as aspirin, that reduces or eliminates pain without affecting consciousness.

**anesthetic**
(n-es-thet' ik)

A drug that causes insensitivity to pain by depressing the central nervous system; used for surgical operations. Anesthetics can be either general or local: general anesthetics are administered to the whole body and produce unconsciousness; local anesthetics are used to anesthetize only the region of the body on which surgery is to be performed.

**antibiotics**
(n-tī-bī-ot' iks)

Medicines, such as penicillin, used to treat bacterial infections.

**anticoagulant**
(n-tī-kō-ag'-lant)

A drug that slows blood clotting (coagulation) and prevents new clots from forming. Anticoagulants are used for the management of stroke and heart disease.

**antihypertensive drug**
(n-tī-hī-per-ten'iv)

A medicine used to lower blood pressure. These drugs sometimes produce side effects, particularly in older patients. Some antihypertensive drugs interact with other drugs—both prescription and over-the-counter medicines.
See hypertension (page 25).

**aspirin**

Aspirin is one of the most frequently used medicines. It can relieve pain, lower fever, reduce inflammation, and prevent the formation of blood clots. However, aspirin sometimes produces adverse effects such as stomach irritation and bleeding. Aspirin is the generic name for the chemical acetylsalicylic acid. Also see generic (page 33).

**barbiturate**
*(bar-bit' $\bar{u}$-rat or bar-bit' ur-it)*

A class of drugs whose major action is a calming or depressant effect on the central nervous system. Barbiturates are used for various purposes, including controlling epileptic seizures and inducing sleep. Barbiturates, like other sedatives, often produce undesirable side effects in older persons such as drowsiness during the day or confusion. See sedative (page 34).

**caffeine**

A drug that stimulates the heart, kidneys, and central nervous system. Caffeine is found in tea, coffee, cola drinks, chocolate, and some over-the-counter drugs.

**diuretic**
*(dī-u-ret' ik)*

A medication that induces the loss of water and salt from the body, used for lowering blood pressure. Common side effects of a diuretic are dehydration and loss of potassium. See hypertension (page 25), dehydration (page 29).

**drug interaction**

Two or more drugs taken simultaneously can produce an unwanted effect or drug interaction. Drug interactions periodically cause problems, but only occasionally cause a problem that may be dangerous. Older persons are more likely to experience drug interactions since they, as a group, use the most drugs.

**eneric**
*e-ner' ick)*

Generic drugs have the same active chemical ingredient as brand name drugs (the trade name given to a drug by its manufacturer). For example, aspirin is the generic name for numerous brand name drugs sold over the counter. Most generic products are less expensive than brand name products, yet are as effective.

**axative**

A preparation that loosens the bowels and eases defecation. Laxatives are ordinarily used to treat constipation; however, overuse may cause constipation as well as other bowel problems.

**ver-the-counter
)TC) drugs**

Nonprescription medicines. OTC drugs are chemicals (like prescription drugs) and are capable of interacting with other OTC drugs, prescription medicines, and alcoholic beverages. Examples are aspirin, laxatives, and vitamins.

**harmacology**
*ar-ma-kol' o-jē)*

The medical science concerned with the development and use of medicines. The field includes medicinal chemistry, experimental therapeutics, and toxicology.

**lacebo**
*la-sē' bō)*

A treatment containing no active component such as pills made only of sugar. Placebos were originally developed for patients who demanded unnecessary medication; later they came to be used for research experiments in evaluating a drug's effectiveness.

33

**psychotropic drugs**
*(sī-kō-trop´ ik)*

Those drugs affecting the mind (psyche) such as tranquilizers.

**sedative**
*(sed´ a-tiv)*

Any drug that quiets excitement or nervousness by depressing the nervous system. Alcohol, tranquilizers, and barbiturates are all sedatives.

**side effect**

Also called adverse effect. A drug response that accompanies the principal response for which a drug is taken. Most side effects are undesirable yet cause only minor annoyance; a few cause serious problems. Elderly persons tend to develop more side effects from medication than young persons.

**toxicity**
*(tok-sis´ i-tē)*

The capacity of a drug to damage body tissue of seriously impair body functions.

# Medical Problems

**alcoholism**

A chronic disease in which repeated episodes of drinking alcoholic beverages cause injury to the individual's health, social functioning, or economic well-being. Alcohol impairs mental alertness, judgment, and physical coordination—further increasing the risk of falls and accidents already common among older people. Moreover, alcohol (which is itself a drug) can produce a wide range of side effects similar to those of prescription and OTC medications. See side effect (page 34).

**arthritis**
(arth-rī′ tis)

A general term referring to disease of the joints. Arthritis includes over 100 different diseases, often involving aches and pains in the joints and connective tissues throughout the body. Most forms of arthritis are chronic, but proper treatment can frequently reduce symptoms substantially. The most common types of arthritis in older persons are osteoarthritis, rheumatoid arthritis, and gout.

***gout.*** An inherited condition, gout usually develops in men between the ages 40 and 60. The condition results from an excess of uric acid in the blood that accumulates in the joints to produce severe inflammation. Years ago, chronic pain and deformity were common characteristics of gout; now medical treatment almost always controls the disease.

*inflammation (in-fla-mā' shun)*. The reaction of the body tissues to injury. Heat, swelling, redness, and pain in the affected area characterize inflammation.

*osteoarthritis (ahs-tē-o-arth-ñ' tis)*. A degenerative joint disease, osteoarthritis usually produces stiffness or pain in the fingers or in weightbearing joints (knees, hips, and spine). Inflammation is rare. While the cause of osteoarthritis is unknown, recent research shows that the cartilage in persons with severe osteoarthritis symptoms is different from the cartilage in persons without symptoms; also, wear and tear on joint surfaces appears to contribute to the condition. Most people over 60 have this type of arthritis but to varying degrees; only about half experience symptoms.

*rheumatism (ru' ma-tiz-um)*. A term used more often in Great Britain. Rheumatism refers to disease in the joints, muscles, bones, and ligaments and includes most forms of arthritis.

*rheumatoid arthritis (ru' ma-toyd)*. The most common form of arthritis after osteoarthritis. It also has the potential for causing the greatest damage since early, mild symptoms can worsen over the years to produce serious deformity. No cause or cure is known. Common symptoms are inflammation in the hands, arms, hips, legs, and feet. The disease affects women more frequently than men.

**cancer**
*(kan' sur)*

A malignant growth or tumor. Cancerous cells grow and reproduce with abnormal speed and can eventually cause death. The two groups of cancers include carcinomas and sarcomas. Carcinomas grow in epithelial (tissue) cells and appear on the skin, colon, stomach, uterus, or breasts; sarcomas grow in the tissues of bones, muscles, or blood vessels. See tumor (page 44).

*biopsy (bī' op-sē).* A medical procedure in which a small piece of tissue is removed for microscopic examination. The procedure is most often used to determine if cells are cancerous.

*oncology (on-kol' o-jē).* The medical study of cancer, including its diagnosis and treatment.

**diabetes**
*(dī-a-bē' tis)*

A disease that prevents the body from using sugar properly. The condition may result from the failure of the pancreas to make enough insulin or the body's inability to respond to the insulin it does have. The most common form in older people is "adult onset" or noninsulin-dependent diabetes. Of 11.5 million diabetics in the U.S., roughly one-third are older persons.

*glucose tolerance test (glu' kōs).* The test measures the level of glucose in the blood before and (at timed intervals) after drinking a special glucose liquid. Recent research shows that some increase occurs in blood glucose levels as people age. Thus, the diagnostic standards for detecting diabetes, formerly based on young persons, are now being revised.

*insulin.* A hormone produced in the pancreas which helps the body metabolize sugar and starches.

**hernia**
*(hur' nē-a)*

The protrusion of an organ or part of an organ beyond its normal space, most often through the abdominal wall.

**hyperthermia**
*(hī-per-thur' mē-a)*

A condition in which the body temperature is so far above normal (e.g., above 104°F or 40°C) that irreversible damage or even death may result. Hyperthermia sometimes appears as heat stroke or heat exhaustion.

**hypoglycemia**
*(hī-pō-glī-sē' mē-a)*

Low blood sugar. An uncommon condition in which glucose (sugar) in the blood is below a normal level. Onset can be sudden and if left untreated, it can lead to confusion, sleepiness, or even unconsciousness. Hypoglycemia is sometimes caused by the overuse of an antidiabetic medicine such as insulin or oral antidiabetic drugs.

**hypothermia**
*(hī-pō-thur' mē-a)*

A condition in which the body temperature drops so far below normal (e.g., below 95⁰F or 35⁰C) that irreversible damage or death may result. Anyone exposed to severe cold can develop accidental hypothermia; however, those at greatest risk are older persons who have chronic illnesses, suffer from temperature-regulation defects, or cannot afford heating fuel.

**influenza**

Also called the "flu." A contagious viral infection that spreads rapidly from person to person. Symptoms include fever, headache, aching muscles, chills, and coughing. Influenza threatens older persons because it lowers their resistance to serious infections like pneumonia.

**insomnia**
*(in-som' nē-a)*

The inability to sleep or unusual wakefulness. Insomnia in the elderly is frequently a manifestation of depression.

**Parkinson's disease**
*(par' kin-sunz)*

A neurological disorder characterized by involuntary muscle tremors and rigid movements. In advanced stages the individual develops a shuffling gait with stooped posture and loses facial expression. The disease occurs most frequently in persons over age 60, striking approximately 1 in 100 persons. The cause of Parkinson's disease is unknown, yet scientists have learned it has to do with a disorder in brain cells that results in the loss of dopamine, a substance regulating normal body movement.

***L-dopa.*** Also called levodopa. L-dopa is a medication used for alleviating symptoms of Parkinson's disease by compensating for the loss of dopamine in the brain.

**pneumonia**
*(nū-mōn' ya)*

Pneumonia is an inflammation of the lungs caused by bacterial infection. Symptoms are similar to influenza but more severe—with fever, coughing, and shaking chills. Pneumonia is one of the five leading causes of death among people over 65.

**progeria**
*(prō-jer' i-a)*

Premature aging. Progeria is a rare condition known also by the name Hutchinson-Gilford progeria syndrome. Signs begin to appear in the individual soon after birth, and the average life expectancy is approximately 12 years.

**syncope**
*(sing' ko-pē)*

Fainting. In older people this is a common cause of falling. See falling (page 42).

# Related Terms:

**acute**
*(a-kūt' )*

Developing rapidly with pronounced symptoms and lasting a short time. One example of an acute illness is the flu (influenza). Compare chronic (page 41).

| | |
|---|---|
| **atrophy**<br>*(a' tro-fē)* | The wasting away of an organ or body part. Atrophy can result when part of the body is not used or, to a lesser extent, in the normal course of aging. |
| **bacteria** | The scientific term for a large group of microscopic, unicellular organisms which can cause disease in man. Some forms of pneumonia, urinary tract infections, and upper respiratory infections are caused by bacteria. Bacterial infections are usually treated with antibiotics. Compare virus (page 44). |
| **biofeedback**<br>*(bī-ō-fēd' bak)* | A technique in which information about a specific body function is given to the individual through visual or auditory displays. Biofeedback techniques are used for learning to control physiological processes, such as urinary incontinence, or to reduce headache pain. |
| **chronic**<br>*(kron' ik)* | Continuing over a long period of time or recurring frequently. Chronic conditions often begin inconspicuously and symptoms are less pronounced than in acute conditions. Compare acute (page 40). |
| **diagnosis**<br>*(dī-ug-nō' sis)* | The process of determining, through examination and analysis, the nature of a patient's illness. |
| **etiology**<br>*(ē-tē-ol' a-jē)* | The study of the cause or origin of a disease. |

41

**falling**

A common problem experienced among older people, due to any number of underlying causes. Evaluating people who have falls involves assessing the injuries sustained in the fall and the cause for the fall. In older people, falling frequently results in broken bones and other serious injuries which may lead to disability and sometimes death.

**homeostatic reserve**
*(hō-mē-o-stat' ik)*

The ability of an organ, an organ system, or an individual to maintain normal body functions. Homeostatic reserve is lowered by illness as well as in the course of normal aging; illness causes the far greater loss in reserve.

**iatrogenic illness**
*(ī-at-ro-jen' ik)*

An illness resulting from some action taken by a health care worker during the process of medical care. For example, the illness may be caused by the efforts of a physician (through the physician's examination, comments, or treatment) or the efforts of a nurse or other health care worker. An iatrogenic illness can also result from an older person's move to an unfamiliar setting such as a nursing home.

**immunity**

The state of being resistant or not susceptible to a disease. Some immunity is natural (e.g., cats and dogs may develop distemper, but humans are naturally immune to this infection); most immunity is produced by the body in the form of specific antibodies (proteins) or by certain blood cells after exposure to antigens (foreign substances such as bacteria or viruses).

**implant** — Transplanted or inserted material—for example, artificial joints used in reconstructive surgery. See prosthetic device (below).

**infection** — An illness caused by an organism such as a virus, bacterium, or fungus.

**intravenous (I.V.)** *(in-tra-vē' nus)* — Within or into the veins.

**nonspecific presentation of illness** — Symptoms appearing in an individual that do not clearly point to a single disease or single organ system. Older persons more than those in other age groups come to the attention of health care providers due to nonspecific reasons.

**prosthetic device** *(pros-thet' ick)* — Sometimes called a prosthesis. Artificial limbs, false teeth, and hearing aids are examples of protheses—all of which augment or replace lost functions of the body. See implant (above).

**risk factors** — Those physical conditions or life habits that increase the likelihood of becoming ill.

**symptom** *(sim' tum)* — The subjective evidence of a patient's condition (pain, shortness of breath, and fainting spells) as opposed to a sign, which is the objective evidence of disease (high blood pressure, a heart murmer, and swollen joints).

**syndrome**
*(sin' drōm)*

A group of symptoms that, together, characterize a particular disease.

**topical**
*(top' i-kul)*

Applied locally or to a particular area of the skin. Topical medications normally affect only the area to which they are applied, although some topical medications (such as estrogen creams) may be absorbed into the bloodstream.

**tumor**
*(tu' mer)*

Also called neoplasm. An abnormal swelling or growth in some part of the body. See cancer (page 37).

*benign (bi-nīn').* Referring to a harmless growth or tumor such as a wart.

*malignant (ma-lig' nant).* Abnormal tissue that can spread (metastasize) to other parts of the body and cause death.

**virus**

An extremely small infectious agent which frequently cannot be seen even under the most sophisticated microscopes. Viruses grow by invading living cells where they replicate. Their replication can cause serious diseases such as influenza, poliomyelitis, and smallpox, as well as minor disorders such as the common cold. Unlike bacterial infections, viral infections cannot be cured or treated with antibiotics. Compare bacteria (page 41).

# Women

**climacteric**
*(klī-mak' ter-ik  or*
*klī-mak-ter' ik)*

Menopause; a period of physical, hormonal, and psychological change. The time when a woman's ability to bear children ends. Also see menopause (page 46).

**estrogen**
*(es' tra-jen)*

A sex hormone that exists primarily in females, although it is also produced in males in limited amounts. Estrogen affects menstruation and development of the reproductive organs (uterus, ovaries, vagina); it is also responsible for secondary female characteristics (breasts).

**gynecology**
*(gī-ne-kol' u-jē)*

The branch of medicine concerned with the health and disorders of the female reproductive system.

**hot flashes or flushes**

During menopause, a transitory sensation of heat similar to blushing but often involving the whole body. Hot flashes occur as blood vessels readjust to diminished amounts of estrogen being produced by the body.

**hysterectomy**
*(his-te-rek' te-mē)*

The surgical removal of the uterus. Total hysterectomy is the removal of the uterus and both ovaries.

**mammography**
*(ma-mog' ra-fē)*

X-ray examination of the breasts to detect abnormal growths, especially cancer. This type of X-ray is often capable of detecting cancer in such early stages it can be cured. The American Cancer Society recommends that women over age 50 have a mammogram annually.

**mastectomy**
*(mas-tek' te-mē)*

The surgical removal of a significant amount of breast tissue.

**menopause**
*(men' o-pauz)*

The permanent cessation of menstruation in the female, taking place usually around age 50. Also see climacteric (page 45).

**ovariectomy or oophorectomy**
*(o-var-i-ek' to-mē; oo-fo-rek' te-mē)*

The surgical removal of one or both ovaries.

**Pap test**

A diagnostic procedure used to detect cancer of the cervix (hollow end of the uterus forming the passageway into the vaginal canal). The test was named for its developer, American anatomist George Papanicolaou. Physicians recommend that the test be included in the regular medical care of women at every age.

# Mental Health

**depression**
*(di-presh' un)*

Feelings of unhappiness, sadness, or despair. Depression is normal and universally experienced, although it can also be a clinical disorder affecting both the physical and mental performance of an individual.

**grief**

A normal emotional response to loss. Grief is usually self-limited and subsides after a reasonable time; on occasion, however, it can transform into depression.

**hypochondria**
*(hi-po-kon' drē-a)*

A neurotic disorder in which afflicted individuals are preoccupied with the worry that they are, or will soon become, physically ill. In elderly persons Hypochondria is frequently a sign of depression.

**intelligence**

The capacity to learn, and the capacity to utilize appropriately what one has learned.

**mental illness**

Any of a number of psychological or behavioral disorders that impair a person's functioning. The cause may be social, psychobiological, genetic, or chemical. Mental illness is usually characterized either as a psychosis or a neurosis. Psychosis is a break with reality so impairing a person's ability to think, remember, communicate, and behave appropriately that it interferes significantly with daily living. Neurosis is any other type of emotional disturbance not diagnosed as a psychosis.

**psychiatry**
*(sī-kī'a-trē)*

The medical specialty concerned with mental or emotional disorders. The psychiatrist is an M.D. or a D.O. trained to diagnose and treat these disorders through a variety of methods, including psychotherapy and medications. Psychiatrists who specialize in working with older people are called geriatric psychiatrists or geropsychiatrists.

**psychosomatic**
*(sī-kō-sō-mat' ik)*

A condition in which a physical illness appears to have an emotional cause. This term points out the close interaction of the mind (psyche) and the body (soma).

**psychotherapy**
*(sī-kō-ther' a-pē)*

The treatment of mental or emotional disorders, usually through verbal communication between patient and therapist.

# Social Programs and Services

**Adult day care**

The social, recreational, and rehabilitation services provided for persons who require daytime supervision. An alternative between care in the home and in an institution.

**Allied health professionals**

Persons with special training in fields related to medicine such as medical social work and physical or occupational therapy. Allied health professionals work with physicians or other health professionals.

**Congregate housing**
*(kong' gra-gat)*

Apartment houses or group accommodations that provide health care and other support services to functionally impaired older persons who do not need routine nursing care.

**Gray lobby**

An advocacy movement whose members are concerned with the needs of the elderly. These individuals come from the general public, organizations of older people (e.g., American Association of Retired Persons, Gray Panthers), and health and welfare professions.

**Home health care**

Health services provided in the homes of the elderly, disabled, sick, or convalescent. The types of services provided include nursing care, social services, home health aide and homemaker services, and various rehabilitation therapies (e.g., speech, physical, and occupational therapy).

| | |
|---|---|
| **homemaker or home health aide** | A person who is paid to help in the home with personal care, light housekeeping, meal preparation, and shopping. Some states and agencies make a distinction between homemaking (or housekeeping) services and personal care services. |
| **hospice** *(hos' pis)* | A concept that refers to enhancing the dying person's quality of life. Hospice care can be given in the home, a special hospice facility, or a combination of both. |
| **institutional-ization** | Admission of an individual to an institution, such as a nursing home, where he or she will reside for an extended period of time or indefinitely. |
| **long-term care** | The medical and social care given to individuals who have severe, chronic impairments. Long-term care can consist of care in the home, by family members, assistance through voluntary or employed help (e.g., as provided by established home care agencies), or care in institutions. Various types of long-term care facilities exist throughout the country which frequently differ in their available staff, reimbursements, and services.

*domiciliary care facility.* A nonmedical institution providing room, board, laundry, some forms of personal care, and usually recreational and social services. Licensed by state departments of social |

services, these facilities are not eligible for Medicare or Medicaid reimbursement.

*intermediate care facility.* Provides health-related care and services to individuals who do not require the degree of care or treatment normally given by a hospital or skilled nursing facility but who do require health-related institutional care above the level of room and board. Eligible for Medicaid reimbursement.

*skilled nursing facility.* Provides the greatest degree of medical care. Every patient is under the supervision of a physician, and the facility has a transfer agreement with a nearby hospital. Twenty-four hour nursing is provided with a physician on-call to furnish medical care in case of emergency. May be covered under both Medicare and Medicaid.

Also see home health care, page 49.

**meals-on-wheels**    A program that delivers meals to the homebound.

**Medicaid**    A national medical assistance program administered by the individual states. Medicaid provides reimbursement for medical and health-related services to persons who are medically indigent. Nursing home care for needy older persons is also covered by Medicaid.

| | |
|---|---|
| **Medicare** | A national health insurance plan for people over 65 and for some people under 65 who are disabled. It includes two parts: part A covers hospital costs and some skilled nursing care, and part B is the supplemental portion (for which the insured pays premiums) covering a portion of the physician's fee as well as various types of therapy. |
| **occupational therapy** | A method of rehabilitation through the teaching of an art or a specific occupation for persons physically or mentally impaired. Such activities are intended to help patients return to their everyday life. |
| **Older Americans Act** | Enacted in 1965 (Public Law 89-73), the purpose of the Older Americans Act is to give elderly citizens more opportunity to participate in and receive the benefits of modern society—for example, adequate housing, income, employment, nutrition, and health care. |
| **physical therapy** | The treatment of disease or impaired motion through a physical method such as heat, hydrotherapy, massage, exercise, or mechanical devices. See rehabilitation therapy (page 53). |
| **physician assistants** | Persons who perform a number of tasks that were traditionally performed by the physician (taking medical histories, making routine examinations). Training for physician assistants usually includes a |

specialized, 2-year program. Physician assistants always work under the supervision of a physician.

**ehabilitation herapy**
*rē-ha-bil-i-tā' shun)*

Therapy aimed at restoring or maintaining the greatest possible function and independence. Rehabilitation therapy is especially useful to persons who have suffered from stroke, an injury, or disease by helping them recover the maximum use of the affected area(s) of the body.

**etirement**

The act of leaving paid employment. The retiree, upon reaching a predetermined age, is usually provided some regular payment such as a pension and/or a Social Security payment.

*flexible retirement.* An employment option allowing an individual to retire at an age of his or her choice.

*mandatory retirement.* The policy of requiring persons to leave employment upon reaching a designated age. This designated age "ceiling" was recently raised by law in the U.S. from age 65 to 70.

**self-help, self-care**

A concept of health care stressing that individuals can manage many of their own health problems when given sufficient instruction and appropriate medications. It teaches how and when to

|                              |                                                                                                                                                                                                                                                                               |
| ---------------------------- | ----------------------------------------------------------------------------------------------------------------------------------------------------------------------------------------------------------------------------------------------------------------------------- |
|                              | use self-treatment techniques and when to seek professional help.                                                                                                                                                                                                              |
| **senior center**            | A community facility for the elderly. Senior centers provide a variety of activities for their members—including any combination of recreational, educational, cultural, or social events. Also, some centers offer nutritious meals and limited health care services.         |
| **Social Security**          | A national insurance program that provides income to workers when they retire or are disabled and to dependent survivors when a worker dies. Retirement payments are based on workers' earnings during employment.                                                             |
| **social services**          | Services designed to help individuals with problems that concern housing, transportation, meals, recreation, and family support and relations. These services are provided by professional social workers.                                                                    |
| **Supplemental Security Income** | This national program provides supplemental payments to older persons who already receive public assistance. The program's aim is to raise the incomes of these individuals to the poverty threshold.                                                                  |

# Medical Specialties

| | |
|---|---|
| **cardiology** | See page 25. |
| **dermatology** | See page 29. |
| **endocrinology** (en-dō-kra-nol' o-jē) | The medical study of the structure, function, and diseases of the endocrine system. This system is made up of glandular tissues (e.g., the pituitary gland, pancreas, sex organs) which secrete hormones directly into the bloodstream to regulate body functions such as growth, sexual development, and emotions. |
| **epidemiology** | See page 12. |
| **family practice** | The physician trained in this specialty gives basic, comprehensive medical care to all members of the family on a continuing basis. Family practitioners perform the same functions as general practitioners did in earlier years. |
| **gastroenterology** | See page 30. |
| **geriatric medicine** | See page 8. |
| **geriatric psychiatry** | See psychiatry, page 48. |
| **gynecology** | See page 45. |
| **hematology** | See page 25. |
| **holistic medicine** | A system of medical care that views the individual as a totality rather than as a collection of separate organs or functions. Interacting variables considered are a patient's physiology, nutrition, |

environment, emotional state, and chosen lifestyle. Holistic medicine relies on the patient becoming educated about his or her own medical care and taking responsible actions to maintain good health.

**internal medicine**

The medical study of the structure, function, and diseases of internal organ systems. Internists are diagnosticians, personal physicians for adult medical care, health counselors, and consultants to other physicians. Many subspecialize in areas such as cardiology, hematology, allergy, and rheumatology.

**nephrology**

See page 27.

**nuclear medicine**
*(nu' klē-ur)*

A branch of radiology that uses nuclear physics to diagnose and treat disease. For example, by circulating radioactive isotopes through the body, certain abnormalities can be made visible on scanning machines. See radiology (page 57).

**ophthalmology**

See page 22.

**optometry**

See page 22.

**orthopedics**

See page 17.

**osteopathic medicine**
*(os-tē-o-path' ik)*

Doctors of osteopathic medicine (D.O.) receive similar training and perform similar functions as medical doctors (M.D.). A special emphasis of the D.O. is on diagnosing and treating structural problems through manipulating the musculoskeletal system.

**pathology**

The medical specialty that studies the cause and effect of disease. The pathologist is an M.D. or D.O. who analyzes biopsied tissue, performs autopsies, and tests blood, urine, and other specimens.

**podiatry**
*(pō-dī′ a-trē)*

The diagnosis and treatment of foot injury or disease. Podiatrists are doctors of podiatric medicine, not M.D.'s or D.O.'s. They make devices to correct problems, provide care for nails, prescribe certain drugs, and perform surgery on the foot.

**preventive medicine**

Program aims are to prevent disease and disability through immunizations, nutrition counseling, health screening, and health education. Usually administered under a department of public health.

**proctology**

See page 30.

**psychiatry**

See page 48.

**radiology**

The medical specialty using X-rays, computerized tomography (CT) scans, radioactive substances, and other similar procedures to diagnose and treat illness.

**rheumatology**

See page 17.

**surgery**

The branch of medicine that treats disease, injury, or deformity by operating on the body. Surgery may involve organ transplants (e.g., a kidney or stomach), implants (heart pacemaker), and prosthetic attachments (an artificial arm or leg). A general surgeon is qualified to perform many common operations but most specialize in one area of the body—for example, neurosurgeons treat disorders relating to the nervous system, spinal cord, and brain.

**urology**

See page 28.

# Index

# Notes